Keto Chaffle Cookbook

Healthy and Delicious only Low-Carb Chaffle Recipes for the Busy Smart People

Sophie Ross

TABLE OF CONTENTS

INTRODUCTION..6

BREAKFAST CHAFFLE RECIPES 10

1. Crispy Chaffles With Egg and Asparagus 10

2. Coconut Chaffles 12

3. Peanut Butter Cup Chaffles..14

4. Chocolaty Chaffles..16

5. Mc Griddle Chaffle 18

6. Cinnamon Swirl Chaffles 20

7. Raspberries Chaffle 22

8. Garlic and Parsley Chaffles.. 24

9. Scrambled Eggs and A Spring Onion Chaffle........................... 26

10. Egg and A Cheddar Cheese Chaffle....................................... 28

LUNCH CHAFFLE RECIPES 31

11. Chicken Bites with Chaffles 31

12. Fish and Chaffle Bites 33

13. Grill Pork Chaffle Sandwich 34

14. Chaffles & Chicken Lunch Plate.. 36

15. Chaffle Egg Sandwich 38

16. Chaffle Minutes Sandwich.. 39

17. Chaffle Cheese Sandwich...42

18. Chicken Zinger Chaffle...43

19. Double Chicken Chaffles...46

DINNER CHAFFLE RECIPES...48

20. Italian Sausage Chaffles...48

21. Chaffles With Strawberry Frosty...49

22. Pecan Pumpkin Chaffle...50

23. Savory Gruyere & Chives Chaffles...51

24. Swiss Bacon Chaffle...53

25. Bacon, Olives & Cheddar Chaffle...54

26. Garlic Chaffle...56

27. Herby Chaffle Snacks...57

28. Zucchini Chaffle...58

BASIC SANDWICH AND CAKE CHAFFLE RECIPES..........60

29. Pecan Pie Cake Chaffle:...60

30. German Chocolate Chaffle Cake:...62

31. Almond Chocolate Chaffle Cake:...64

32. Peanut Butter Keto Chaffle Cake...66

33. Italian Cream Chaffle Cake...68

34. Banana Cake Pudding Chaffle...70

35. Cream Coconut Chaffle Cake...72

36. Fluffy White Chaffles 74

37. Blueberry Keto Chaffle 75

38. Keto Birthday Cake Chaffle Recipe with Sprinkles 77

DESSERT CHAFFLE RECIPES 80

39. Italian Cream Chaffle Sandwich-cake 80

40. Whipping Cream Chaffle... 82

41. Cinnamon Pumpkin Chaffles 83

42. Red Velvet Chaffles 84

43. Mayonnaise Chaffles 86

44. Chocolate Peanut Butter Chaffle...................................... 87

45. Lemon Curd Chaffles 88

46. Walnut Pumpkin Chaffles 90

47. Protein Mozzarella Chaffles 91

48. Chocolate Chips Peanut Butter Chaffles............................ 93

49. Dessert Pumpkin Chaffles... 95

50. Lemon Chaffles... 96

CONCLUSION 98

INTRODUCTION

If you enjoy desserts like I do, you may enjoy the book. I will share some of my favorite keto chaffle recipes in this book. This is a great way to have your cake and eat it too without any guilt!

What are chaffles?

Chaffles are low carb, low calorie and high in protein- perfect for anyone on a weight-loss plan or diet. If you've been wondering how to lose weight without sacrificing taste, these yummy creations may be just what the doctor ordered! Chaffles make for a satisfying meal that doesn't leave you feeling guilty about indulging in something sweet. Chaffles are the perfect solution for those looking to stay within their carb/calorie limits. They are reminiscent of pancakes but taste similar to a waffle due to the texture. These 'cakes' can be made in advance and heated up whenever you get hungry, making them great for busy lifestyles!

They can even be frozen so you can enjoy them at any time of the day!

They're best when served warm with a drizzle of low-fat cream cheese, butter or sugar-free ice cream.

They are also great toasted with sugar-free maple syrup.

Why is chaffles perfect for someone who is into Ketogenic Diet?

Here are several reasons:

1. Chaffles are made with almond flour and coconut flour, which are both low-carb flours.
2. They contain 0 carb, making them perfect for diabetics and those following a Ketogenic Diet (such as Atkins Diet).
3. Chaffles are low in calories but high in protein due to the whey protein powder they contain.
4. You can make the batter well ahead of time and refrigerate for up to a week or freeze to bake at a later date- it's perfect for hectic lifestyles!
5. Chaffles can be made savory or sweet according to your preference, so you don't need to have one dessert for sweet tooth and another if you prefer savory food!
6. Chaffles can be made dairy-free by substituting the butter or cream cheese with a non-dairy alternative such as coconut oil.
7. They are perfect for those who enjoy baking but are limited by time constraints, as you can make the batter ahead and refrigerate or freeze for later use!
8. Chaffles have a fluffy texture that is reminiscent of pancakes and waffles, but they're not too dense and don't leave you feeling stuffed after eating one!
9. Chaffles are versatile! You can top them with anything you want, from sugar-free syrup to chocolate chips to low-fat cream cheese or butter.
10. Chaffles are fun to prepare for the kids! Make them in fun shapes and let the kids top them however they want with your favorite low-calorie toppings.

11. Chaffles are egg-free, which is great for those who are allergic to eggs or simply don't like eating eggs!

12. Chaffles are relatively easy to make, although you do need a mixer to properly blend the batter. The rest of the steps are simple and don't require much effort from you!

13. If you love baking but hate doing dishes, chaffles will be perfect for you because they only require one mixing bowl (and a small one at that) and a microwave or oven to heat up!

Now, let us begin with these mouthwatering keto chaffle recipes

BREAKFAST CHAFFLE RECIPES

1. Crispy Chaffles With Egg and Asparagus

Preparation Time: 15 min

Cooking Time: 10 min

Servings: 1

Ingredients:

- 1 egg
- 1/4 cup cheddar cheese
- 2 tbsps. almond flour
- ½ tsp. baking powder
- 1 egg
- 4-5 stalks asparagus
- 1 tsp. avocado oil

Directions:

1. Preheat waffle maker to medium-high heat.
2. Whisk together egg, Mozzarella cheese, almond flour, and baking powder

3. Pour chaffles mixture into the center of the waffle iron. Close the waffle maker and let cooking for 3-5 minutes or until waffle is golden brown and set.
4. Remove chaffles from the waffle maker and serve.
5. Meanwhile, heat oil in a nonstick pan.
6. Once the pan is hot, fry asparagus for about 4-5 minutes until golden brown.
7. Poach the egg in boil water for about 2-3 minutes.
8. Once chaffles are cooked, remove from the maker.
9. Serve chaffles with the poached egg and asparagus.

Nutrition: Calories: 287 kcal Total Fat: 19g Total Carbs: 6.5g Protein: 6.8g

2. Coconut Chaffles

Preparation Time: 10 minutes

Cooking Time: 5 minutes

Servings: 2

Ingredients:

- 1 egg
- 1 oz. cream cheese,
- 1 oz. cheddar cheese
- 2 tbsps. coconut flour
- 1 tsp. stevia
- 1 tbsp. coconut oil, melted
- 1/2 tsp. coconut extract
- 2 eggs, soft boil for serving

Directions:

1. Heat your waffle maker and grease with cooking spray.
2. Mix together all chaffles ingredients in a bowl.
3. Pour chaffle batter in a preheated waffle maker.
4. Close the lid.
5. Cooking chaffles for about 2-3 minutes until golden brown.

6. Serve with boil egg and enjoy

Nutrition: Calories: 331 kcal Protein: 11.84 g Fat: 30.92 g Carbohydrates: 1.06g

3. Peanut Butter Cup Chaffles

Preparation Time: 5 minutes

Cooking Time: 15 minutes

Servings: 1

Ingredients:

For the chaffle:

- Eggs: 1
- Mozzarella cheese: ½ cup shredded
- Cocoa powder: 2 tbsp.
- Espresso powder: ¼ tsp.
- Sugar free chocolate chips: 1 tbsp.

For the filling:

- Peanut butter: 3 tbsp.
- Butter: 1 tbsp.
- Powdered sweetener: 2 tbsp.

Direction:

1. Add all the chaffle ingredients in a bowl and whisk
2. Preheat your mini waffle iron if needed and grease it

3. Cooking your mixture in the mini waffle iron for at least 4 minutes
4. Make two chaffles
5. Mix the filling ingredients together
6. When chaffles cool down, spread peanut butter on them to make a sandwich

Nutrition: Calories: 448; Total Fat: 34g; Carbs: 17g; Net Carbs: 10g; Fiber: 7g; Protein: 24g

4. Chocolaty Chaffles

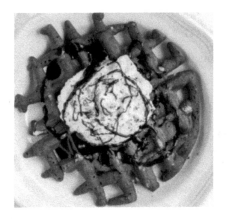

Preparation Time: 5 minutes

Cooking Time: 15 minutes

Servings: 1

Ingredients:

- Eggs: 1
- Mozzarella cheese: ½ cup shredded
- Cocoa powder: 2 tbsp.
- Espresso powder: ¼ tsp.
- Sugar free chocolate chips: 1 tbsp.

Directions:

1. Add all the chaffle ingredients in a bowl and whisk
2. Preheat your mini waffle iron if needed and grease it
3. Cooking your mixture in the mini waffle iron for at least 4 minutes
4. Make as many chaffles as you can

Nutrition: Calories: 258; Total Fat: 23g; Carbs: 12g; Net Carbs: 6g; Fiber: 6g; Protein: 5g

5. Mc Griddle Chaffle

Preparation Time: 5 minutes

Cooking Time: 10 minutes

Servings: 2

Ingredients:

- Egg: 2
- Mozzarella cheese: 1½ cup (shredded)
- Maple Syrup: 2 tbsp. (sugar-free)
- Sausage patty: 2
- American cheese: 2 slices
- Swerve/Monkfruit: 2 tbsp.

Directions:

1. Preheat a mini waffle maker if needed and grease it
2. In a mixing bowl, beat eggs and add shredded Mozzarella cheese, Swerve/Monkfruit, and maple syrup
3. Mix them all well and pour the mixture to the lower plate of the waffle maker
4. Close the lid
5. Cooking for at least 4 minutes to get the desired crunch
6. Remove the chaffle from the heat

7. sausage patty by following the instruction given on the packaging
8. Place a cheese slice on the patty immediately when removing from heat
9. Take two chaffles and put sausage patty and cheese in between
10. Make as many chaffles as your mixture and waffle maker allow
11. Serve hot and enjoy!

Nutrition: Calories: 231; Total Fat: 20g; Carbs: 8g; Net Carbs: 6g; Fiber: 2g; Protein: 9g

6. Cinnamon Swirl Chaffles

Preparation Time: 5 minutes

Cooking Time: 10 minutes

Servings: 2

Ingredients:

For Chaffle:

- Egg: 2
- Cream Cheese: 2 oz. softened
- Almond flour: 2 tbsp.
- Vanilla Extract: 2 tsp.
- Cinnamon: 2 tsp.
- Vanilla extract: 2 tsp.
- Splenda: 2 tbsp.

For Icing:

- Cream cheese: 2 oz. softened
- Splenda: 2 tbsp.
- Vanilla: 1 tsp.
- Butter: 2 tbsp. unsalted butter

For Cinnamon Drizzle:

- Splenda: 2 tbsp.
- Butter: 1 tbsp.
- Cinnamon: 2 tsp.

Directions:

1. Preheat the waffle maker
2. Grease it lightly

3. Mix all the chaffle ingredients together
4. Pour the mixture to the waffle maker
5. Cooking for around 4 minutes or till chaffles become crispy
6. Keep them aside when done
7. In a small bowl, mix the ingredients of icing and cinnamon drizzle
8. Heat it in a microwave for about 10 seconds to gain a soft uniformity
9. Whirl on cooled chaffles and enjoy!

Nutrition: Calories: 323; Total Fat: 27g; Carbs: 8g; Net Carbs: 3g;

Fiber: 5g; Protein: 15g

7. Raspberries Chaffle

Preparation time: 15 minutes

Cooking Time: 15 Minutes

Servings: 1

Ingredients:

- 1 egg white
- 1/4 cup jack cheese, shredded
- 1/4 cup cheddar cheese, shredded
- 1 tsp. coconut flour
- 1/4 tsp. baking powder
- 1/2 tsp. stevia

For Topping

- 4 oz. raspberries
- 2 tbsps. coconut flour
- 2 oz. unsweetened raspberry sauce

Directions:

1. Switch on your round Waffle Maker and grease it with cooking spray once it is hot.
2. Mix together all chaffle ingredients in a bowl and combine with a fork.
3. Pour chaffle batter in a preheated maker and close the lid.
4. Roll the taco chaffle around using a kitchen roller, set it aside and allow it to set for a few minutes.
5. Once the taco chaffle is set, remove from the roller.
6. Dip raspberries in sauce and arrange on taco chaffle.

7. Drizzle coconut flour on top.
8. Enjoy raspberries taco chaffle with keto coffee.

Nutrition: Calories: 386; Total Fat: 37g; Carbs: 13g; Net Carbs: 8g;

Fiber: 5g; Protein: 5g

8. Garlic and Parsley Chaffles

Preparation time: 10 minutes

Cooking Time: 5 Minutes

Servings: 1

Ingredients:

- 1 large egg
- 1/4 cup cheese Mozzarella
- 1 tsp. coconut flour
- ¼ tsp. baking powder
- ½ tsp. garlic powder
- 1 tbsp. minute sced parsley

For Serving

- 1 Poach egg
- 4 oz. smoked salmon

Directions:

1. Switch on your Dash waffle maker and let it preheat.
2. Grease waffle maker with cooking spray.
3. Mix together egg, mozzarella, coconut flour, and baking powder, and garlic powder, parsley to a mixing bowl until combined well.
4. Pour batter in circle chaffle maker.
5. Close the lid.
6. Cooking for about 2-3 minutes or until the chaffles is cooked.
7. Serve with smoked salmon and poached egg.
8. Enjoy!

Nutrition: Calories: 757; Total Fat: 38g; Carbs: 17g; Net Carbs: 11g;

Fiber: 6g; Protein: 29g

9. Scrambled Eggs and A Spring Onion Chaffle

Preparation time: 10 minutes

Cooking Time: 7–9 Minutes

Servings: 4

Ingredients:

Batter

- 4 eggs
- 2 cups grated Mozzarella cheese
- 2 spring onions, finely chopped
- Salt and pepper to taste
- ½ teaspoon dried garlic powder
- 2 tablespoons almond flour
- 2 tablespoons coconut flour

Other

- 2 tablespoons butter for brushing the waffle maker
- 6-8 eggs
- Salt and pepper
- 1 teaspoon Italian spice mix
- 1 tablespoon olive oil
- 1 tablespoon freshly chopped parsley

Directions:

1. Preheat the waffle maker.
2. Crack the eggs into a bowl and add the grated cheese.

3. Mix until just combined, then add the chopped spring onions and season with salt and pepper and dried garlic powder.
4. Stir in the almond flour and mix until everything is combined.
5. Brush the heated waffle maker with butter and add a few tablespoons of the batter.
6. Close the lid and cooking for about 7–8 minutes depending on your waffle maker.
7. While the chaffles are cooking, the scrambled eggs by whisking the eggs in a bowl until frothy, about 2 minutes. Season with salt and black pepper to taste and add the Italian spice mix. Whisk to blend in the spices.
8. Warm the oil in a non-stick pan over medium heat.
9. Pour the eggs in the pan and cooking until eggs are set to your liking.
10. Serve each chaffle and top with some scrambled eggs. Top with freshly chopped parsley.

Nutrition: Calories: 165; Total Fat: 15g; Carbs: 4g; Net Carbs: 2g;

Fiber: 2g; Protein: 6g

10. Egg and A Cheddar Cheese Chaffle

Preparation time: 10 minutes

Cooking Time: 7–9 Minutes

Servings: 4

Ingredients:

Batter

- 4 eggs
- 2 cups shredded white cheddar cheese
- Salt and pepper to taste

Other

- 2 tablespoons butter for brushing the waffle maker
- 4 large eggs
- 2 tablespoons olive oil

Directions:

1. Preheat the waffle maker.
2. Crack the eggs into a bowl and whisk them with a fork.
3. Stir in the grated cheddar cheese and season with salt and pepper.
4. Brush the heated waffle maker with butter and add a few tablespoons of the batter.
5. Close the lid and cooking for about 7–8 minutes depending on your waffle maker.
6. While chaffles are cooking, cooking the eggs.
7. Warm the oil in a large non-stick pan that has a lid over medium-low heat for 2-3 minutes

8. Crack an egg in a small ramekin and gently add it to the pan. Repeat the same way for the other 3 eggs.
9. Cover and let cooking for 2 to 2 ½ minutes for set eggs but with runny yolks.
10. Remove from heat.
11. To serve, place a chaffle on each plate and top with an egg. Season with salt and black pepper to taste.

Nutrition: Calories: 74; Total Fat: 7g; Carbs: 1g; Net Carbs: 0g; Fiber: 0g; Protein: 3g

LUNCH CHAFFLE RECIPES

11. Chicken Bites with Chaffles

Preparation time: 10 minutes

Cooking Time: 10 minutes

Servings: 2

Ingredients:

- 1 chicken breasts cut into 2 x2 inch chunks
- 1 egg, whisked
- 1/4 cup almond flour
- 2 tbsps. onion powder
- 2 tbsps. garlic powder
- 1 tsp. dried oregano
- 1 tsp. paprika powder
- 1 tsp. salt
- 1/2 tsp. black pepper
- 2 tbsps. avocado oil

Directions:

1. Add all the dry ingredients together into a large bowl. Mix well.
2. Place the eggs into a separate bowl.
3. Dip each chicken piece into the egg and then into the dry ingredients.
4. Heat oil in 10-inch skillet, add oil.

5. Once avocado oil is hot, place the coated chicken nuggets onto a skillet and cook for 6-8 minutes Utes until cooked and golden brown.
6. Serve with chaffles and raspberries.
7. Enjoy!

Nutrition: Total Calories 401 kcal Fats 219 g Protein 32.35 g Nectars 1.46 g Fiber 3 g

12. Fish and Chaffle Bites

Preparation time: 10 minutes

Cooking Time: 15 minutes

Servings: 2

Ingredients:

- 1 lb. cod fillets, sliced into 4 slices
- 1 tsp. sea salt
- 1 tsp. garlic powder
- 1 egg, whisked
- 1 cup almond flour
- 2 tbsp. avocado oil

Chaffle Ingredients:

- 2 eggs
- 1/2 cup cheddar cheese
- 2 tbsps. almond flour
- ½ tsp. Italian seasoning

Directions:

1. Mix together chaffle ingredients in a bowl and make 4 squares
2. Put the chaffles in a preheated chaffle maker.
3. Mix together the salt, pepper, and garlic powder in a mixing bowl. Toss the cod cubes in this mixture and let sit for 10 minutes Utes.
4. Then dip each cod slice into the egg mixture and then into the almond flour.

5. Heat oil in skillet and fish cubes for about 2-3 minutes Utes, until cooked and browned
6. Serve on chaffles and enjoy!

Nutrition: Protein: 38% 121 kcal Fat: 59% 189 kcal Carbohydrates: 3% 11 kcal

13. Grill Pork Chaffle Sandwich

Preparation time: 10 minutes

Cooking Time: 15 Minutes

Servings:2

Ingredients:

- 1/2 cup mozzarella, shredded
- 1 egg
- I pinch garlic powder

Pork Patty

- 1/2 cup pork, minutes
- 1 tbsp. green onion, diced
- 1/2 tsp Italian seasoning
- Lettuce leaves

Directions:

1. Preheat the square waffle maker and grease with
2. Mix together egg, cheese and garlic powder in a small mixing bowl.
3. Pour batter in a preheated waffle maker and close the lid.
4. Make 2 chaffles from this batter.

5. Cook chaffles for about 2-3 minutes Utes until cooked through.
6. Meanwhile, mix together pork patty ingredients in a bowl and make 1 large patty.
7. Grill pork patty in a preheated grill for about 3-4 minutes Utes per side until cooked through.
8. Arrange pork patty between two chaffles with lettuce leaves. Cut sandwich to make a triangular sandwich.
9. Enjoy!

Nutrition: Protein: 48% 85 kcal Fat: 48% 86 kcal Carbohydrates: 4% 7 kcal

14. <u>Chaffles & Chicken Lunch Plate</u>

Preparation time: 10 minutes

Cooking Time: 15 Minutes

Servings:2

Ingredients:

- 1 large egg
- 1/2 cup jack cheese, shredded
- 1 pinch salt

For Serving

- 1 chicken leg
- salt
- pepper
- 1 tsp. garlic, minutes
- 1 egg
- 1 tsp avocado oil

Directions:

1. Heat your square waffle maker and grease with cooking spray.
2. Pour Chaffle batter into the skillet and cook for about 3 minutes Utes.
3. Meanwhile, heat oil in a pan, over medium heat.
4. Once the oil is hot, add chicken thigh and garlic then, cook for about 5 minutes Utes. Flip and cook for another 3-4 minutes.
5. Season with salt and pepper and give them a good mix.
6. Transfer cooked thigh to plate.

7. Fry the egg in the same pan for about 1-2 minutes Utes according to your choice.

8. Once chaffles are cooked, serve with fried egg and chicken thigh.

9. Enjoy!

Nutrition: Protein: 31% 138 kcal Fat: 66% 292 kcal Carbohydrates: 2% kcal

15. Chaffle Egg Sandwich

Preparation time: 10 minutes

Cooking Time: 10 Minutes

Servings:2

Ingredients:

- 2 keto chaffle
- 2 slice cheddar cheese
- 1 egg simple omelet

Directions:

1. Prepare your oven on 4000 F.
2. Arrange egg omelet and cheese slice between chaffles.
3. Bake in the preheated oven for about 4-5 minutes Utes until cheese is melted.
4. Once the cheese is melted, remove from the oven.
5. Serve and enjoy!

Nutrition: Protein: 29% 144 kcal Fat: % 337 kcal Carbohydrates: 3% 14 kcal

16. Chaffle Minutes Sandwich

Preparation time: 10 minutes

Cooking Time: 10 Minutes

Servings:2

Ingredients:

- 1 large egg
- 1/8 cup almond flour
- 1/2 tsp. garlic powder
- 3/4 tsp. baking powder
- 1/2 cup shredded cheese

Sandwich Filling

- 2 slices deli ham
- 2 slices tomatoes
- 1 slice cheddar cheese

Directions:

1. Grease your square waffle maker and preheat it on medium heat.
2. Mix together chaffle ingredients in a mixing bowl until well combined.
3. Pour batter into a square waffle and make two chaffles.
4. Once chaffles are cooked, remove from the maker.
5. For a sandwich, arrange deli ham, tomato slice and cheddar cheese between two chaffles.
6. Cut sandwich from the center.
7. Serve and enjoy!

Nutrition: Protein: 29% 70 kcal Fat: 66% 159 kcal Carbohydrates: 4% 10 kcal

17. Chaffle Cheese Sandwich

Preparation time: 10 minutes

Cooking Time: 10 Minutes

Servings: 1

Ingredients:

- 2 square keto chaffle
- 2 slice cheddar cheese
- 2 lettuce leaves

Directions:

1. Prepare your oven on 4000 F.
2. Arrange lettuce leave and cheese slice between chaffles.
3. Bake in the preheated oven for about 4-5 minutes Utes until cheese is melted.
4. Once the cheese is melted, remove from the oven.
5. Serve and enjoy!

Nutrition: Protein: 28% kcal Fat: 69% 149 kcal Carbohydrates: 3% 6 kcal

18. Chicken Zinger Chaffle

Preparation time: 10 minutes

Cooking Time: 15 Minutes

Servings:2

Ingredients:

- 1 chicken breast, cut into 2 pieces
- 1/2 cup coconut flour
- 1/4 cup finely grated Parmesan
- 1 tsp. paprika
- 1/2 tsp. garlic powder
- 1/2 tsp. onion powder
- 1 tsp. salt& pepper
- 1 egg beaten
- Avocado oil for frying
- Lettuce leaves
- BBQ sauce

Chaffle Ingredients:

- 4 oz. cheese
- 2 whole eggs
- 2 oz. almond flour
- 1/4 cup almond flour
- 1 tsp baking powder

Directions:

1. Mix together chaffle ingredients in a bowl.
2. Pour the chaffle batter in preheated greased square chaffle maker.

3. Cook chaffles for about 2-minutesutes until cooked through.
4. Make square chaffles from this batter.
5. Meanwhile mix together coconut flour, parmesan, paprika, garlic powder, onion powder salt and pepper in a bowl.
6. Dip chicken first in coconut flour mixture then in beaten egg.
7. Heat avocado oil in a skillet and cook chicken from both sides. until lightly brown and cooked
8. Set chicken zinger between two chaffles with lettuce and BBQ sauce.
9. Enjoy!

Nutrition: Protein: 30% 219 kcal Fat: 60% 435 kcal Carbohydrates: 9% 66 kcal

19. Double Chicken Chaffles

Preparation time: 10 minutes

Cooking Time: 5 Minutes

Servings:2

Ingredients:

- 1/2 cup boil shredded chicken
- 1/4 cup cheddar cheese
- 1/8 cup parmesan cheese
- 1 egg
- 1 tsp. Italian seasoning
- 1/8 tsp. garlic powder
- 1 tsp. cream cheese

Directions:

1. Preheat the Belgian waffle maker.
2. Mix together in chaffle ingredients in a bowl and mix together.
3. Sprinkle 1 tbsp. of cheese in a waffle maker and pour in chaffle batter.
4. Pour 1 tbsp. of cheese over batter and close the lid.
5. Cook chaffles for about 4 to minutes Utes.
6. Serve with a chicken zinger and enjoy the double chicken flavor.

Nutrition: Protein: 30% 60 kcal Fat: 65% 129 kcal Carbohydrates: 5% 9 kcal

DINNER CHAFFLE RECIPES

20. Italian Sausage Chaffles

Preparation time: 10 minutes

Cooking Time: 8 Minutes

Servings: 2

Ingredients:

- 1 egg, beaten
- 1 cup cheddar cheese, shredded
- ¼ cup Parmesan cheese, grated
- 1 lb. Italian sausage, crumbled
- 2 teaspoons baking powder
- 1 cup almond flour

Directions:

1. Preheat your waffle maker.
2. Mix all the ingredients in a bowl.
3. Pour half of the mixture into the waffle maker.
4. Cover and cooking for minutes.
5. Transfer to a plate.
6. Let cool to make it crispy.
7. Do the same steps to make the next chaffle.

Nutrition: Carbohydrates: 1 g Fats: 62 g Proteins: 28 g Calories: 680

21. Chaffles With Strawberry Frosty

Preparation time: 10 minutes

Cooking Time: 5 Minutes

Servings:2

Ingredients:

- 1 cup frozen strawberries
- 1/2 cup Heavy cream
- 1 tsp. stevia
- 1 scoop protein powder
- 3 keto chaffles

Directions:

1. Mix together all ingredients in a mixing bowl.
2. Pour mixture in silicone molds and freeze in a freezer for about 4 hours to set.
3. Once frosty is set, top on keto chaffles and enjoy!

Nutrition: Carbohydrates: 9 g Fats: 36 g Proteins: 32 g Calories: 474

22. Pecan Pumpkin Chaffle

Preparation time: 20 minutes

Cooking Time: 15 Minutes

Servings: 2

Ingredients:

- 1 egg
- 2 tbsp. pecans, toasted and chopped
- 2 tbsp. almond flour
- 1 tsp. erythritol
- 1/4 tsp. pumpkin pie spice
- 1 tbsp. pumpkin puree
- 1/2 cup Mozzarella cheese, grated

Directions:

1. Preheat your waffle maker.
2. Beat egg in a small bowl.
3. Add remaining ingredients and mix well.
4. Spray waffle maker with cooking spray.
5. Pour half batter in the hot waffle maker and cooking for minutes or until golden brown. Repeat with the remaining batter.
6. Serve and enjoy.

Nutrition: Calories: 240 Total Fat: 16 g Protein: 21 g Total Carbs: 3g

Fiber: 1g Net Carbs: 2g

23. Savory Gruyere & Chives Chaffles

Preparation time: 20 minutes

Cooking Time: 14 Minutes

Servings: 2

Ingredients:

- 2 eggs, beaten
- 1 cup finely grated Gruyere cheese
- 2 tbsp. finely grated cheddar cheese
- 1/8 tsp. freshly ground black pepper
- 3 tbsp. minced fresh chives + more for garnishing
- 2 sunshine fried eggs for topping

Directions:

1. Preheat the waffle iron.
2. In a medium bowl, mix the eggs, cheeses, black pepper, and chives.
3. Open the iron and pour in half of the mixture.
4. Close the iron and cooking until brown and crispy, 7 minutes.
5. Remove the chaffle onto a plate and set aside.
6. Make another chaffle using the remaining mixture.
7. Top each chaffle with one fried egg each, garnish with the chives and serve.

Nutrition: Calories: 402 Total Fat: 30g Protein: 30g Total Carbs: 3g Fiber: 1g Net Carbs: 2g

24. Swiss Bacon Chaffle

Preparation time: 10 minutes

Cooking Time: 8 Minutes

Servings: 2

Ingredients:

- 1 egg
- ½ cup Swiss cheese
- 2 tablespoons cooked crumbled bacon

Directions:

1. Preheat your waffle maker.
2. Beat the egg in a bowl.
3. Stir in the cheese and bacon.
4. Pour half of the mixture into the device.
5. Close and cooking for 4 minutes.
6. Cooking the second chaffle using the same steps.

Nutrition: Calories: 317 Total Fat: 18g Protein: 38g Total Carbs: 0g

Fiber: 0g Net Carbs: 0g

25. Bacon, Olives & Cheddar Chaffle

Preparation time: 10 minutes

Cooking Time: 8 Minutes

Servings: 2

Ingredients:

- 1 egg
- ½ cup cheddar cheese, shredded
- 1 tablespoon black olives, chopped
- 1 tablespoon bacon bits

Directions:

1. Plug in your waffle maker.
2. In a bowl, beat the egg and stir in the cheese.
3. Add the black olives and bacon bits.
4. Mix well.
5. Add half of the mixture into the waffle maker.
6. Cover and cooking for 4 minutes.
7. Open and transfer to a plate.
8. Let cool for 2 minutes.
9. Cooking the other chaffle using the remaining batter.

Nutrition: Calories: 733 Total Fat: 53g Protein: 54g Total Carbs: 10g

Fiber: 6g Net Carbs: 4g

26. Garlic Chaffle

Servings: 2

Cooking Time: 8 Minutes

Ingredients:

- 1 egg
- ½ cup cheddar cheese, beaten
- 1 teaspoon coconut flour
- Pinch garlic powder

Directions:

1. Plug in your waffle maker.
2. Beat the egg in a bowl.
3. Stir in the rest of the ingredients.
4. Pour half of the batter into your waffle maker.
5. Cooking for 4 minutes.
6. Remove the waffle and let sit for 2 minutes.
7. Do the same steps with the remaining batter.

Nutrition: Calories 273, Carbs 5.7 g, Fat 12 g, Protein 34 g, Sodium 689 mg, Sugar 0 g

27. Herby Chaffle Snacks

Preparation time: 30 minutes

Cooking Time: 28 Minutes

Servings: 4

Ingredients:

- 1 egg, beaten
- ½ cup finely grated Monterey Jack cheese
- ¼ cup finely grated Parmesan cheese
- ½ tsp. dried mixed herbs

Directions:

1. Preheat the waffle iron.
2. Mix all the ingredients in a medium bowl
3. Open the iron and pour in a quarter of the mixture. Close and cooking until crispy, 7 minutes.
4. Remove the chaffle onto a plate and make 3 more with the rest of the ingredients.
5. Cut each chaffle into wedges and plate.
6. Allow cooling and serve.

Nutrition: Calories 203, Carbs 4.7 g, Fat 10 g, Protein 25 g, Sodium 479 mg, Sugar 0 g

28. Zucchini Chaffle

Preparation time: 10 minutes

Cooking Time: 8 Minutes

Servings: 2

Ingredients:

- 1 cup zucchini, grated
- ¼ cup Mozzarella cheese, shredded
- 1 egg, beaten
- ½ cup Parmesan cheese, shredded
- 1 teaspoon dried basil
- Salt and pepper to taste

Directions:

1. Preheat your waffle maker.
2. Sprinkle pinch of salt over the zucchini and mix.
3. Let sit for 2 minutes.
4. Wrap zucchini with paper towel and squeeze to get rid of water.
5. Transfer to a bowl and stir in the rest of the ingredients.
6. Pour half of the mixture into the waffle maker.
7. Close the device.
8. Cooking for 4 minutes.
9. Make the second chaffle following the same steps.

Nutrition: Calories 273, Carbs 6 g, Fat 11 g, Protein 37 g, Sodium 714 mg, Sugar 0 g

BASIC SANDWICH AND CAKE CHAFFLE RECIPES

29. Pecan Pie Cake Chaffle:

Preparation Time: 15 minutes

Cooking Time: 25 minutes

Servings: 2

Ingredients:

For Pecan Pie Chaffle:

- Egg: 1
- Cream cheese: 2 tbsp.
- Maple extract: ½ tbsp.
- Almond flour: 4 tbsp.
- Sukrin Gold: 1 tbsp.
- Baking powder: ½ tbsp.
- Pecan: 2 tbsp. chopped
- Heavy whipping cream: 1 tbsp.

For Pecan Pie Filling:

- Butter: 2 tbsp.
- Sukrin Gold: 1 tbsp.
- Pecan: 2 tbsp. chopped
- Heavy whipping cream: 2 tbsp.
- Maple syrup: 2 tbsp.
- Egg yolk: 2 large
- Salt: a pinch

Directions:

1. In a small saucepan, add sweetener, butter, syrups, and heavy whipping cream and use a low flame to heat
2. Mix all the ingredients well together
3. Remove from heat and add egg yolks and mix
4. Now put it on heat again and stir
5. Add pecan and salt to the mixture and let it simmer
6. It will thicken then remove from heat and let it rest
7. For the chaffles, add all the ingredients except pecans and blend
8. Now add pecan with a spoon
9. Preheat a mini waffle maker if needed and grease it
10. Pour the mixture to the lower plate of the waffle maker and spread it evenly to cover the plate properly and close the lid
11. Cooking for at least 4 minutes to get the desired crunch
12. Remove the chaffle from the heat and keep aside for around one minute
13. Make as many chaffles as your mixture and waffle maker allow
14. Add 1/3 the previously prepared pecan pie filling to the chaffle and arrange like a cake

Nutrition: Calories: 205 Fat: 2 g Protein: 13 g Carbs: 31 g Fiber: 17g

30. German Chocolate Chaffle Cake:

Preparation Time: 5 minutes

Cooking Time: 10 minutes

Servings: 2

Ingredients:

For Chocolate Chaffle:

- Egg: 1
- Cream cheese: 2 tbsp.
- Powdered sweetener: 1 tbsp.
- Vanilla extract: ½ tbsp.
- Instant coffee powder: ¼ tsp.
- Almond flour: 1 tbsp.
- Cocoa powder: 1 tbsp. (unsweetened)

For Filling:

- Egg Yolk: 1
- Heavy cream: ¼ cup
- Butter: 1 tbsp.
- Powdered sweetener: 2 tbsp.
- Caramel: ½ tsp.
- Coconut flakes: ¼ cup
- Coconut flour: 1 tsp.
- Pecans: ¼ cups chopped

Directions:

1. Preheat a mini waffle maker if needed and grease it
2. In a mixing bowl, beat eggs and add the remaining chaffle ingredients

3. Mix them all well
4. Pour the mixture to the lower plate of the waffle maker and spread it evenly to cover the plate properly and close the lid
5. Cooking for at least 4 minutes to get the desired crunch
6. Remove the chaffle from the heat and let them cool completely
7. Make as many chaffles as your mixture and waffle maker allow
8. In a small pan, mix heavy cream, egg yolk, sweetener, and butter at low heat for around 5 minutes
9. Remove from heat and add the remaining ingredients to make the filling
10. Stack chaffles on one another and add filling in between to enjoy the cake

Nutrition: Calories: 260 Fat: 9 g Protein: 9 g Carbs: 36 g Fiber: 5g

31. Almond Chocolate Chaffle Cake:

Preparation Time: 5 minutes

Cooking Time: 10 minutes

Servings: 2

Ingredients:

For Chocolate Chaffle:

- Egg: 1
- Cream cheese: 2 tbsp.
- Powdered sweetener: 1 tbsp.
- Vanilla extract: ½ tbsp.
- Instant coffee powder: ¼ tsp.
- Almond flour: 1 tbsp.
- Cocoa powder: 1 tbsp. (unsweetened)

For Coconut Filling:

- Melted Coconut Oil: 1 ½ tbsp.
- Heavy cream: 1 tbsp.
- Cream cheese: 4 tbsp.
- Powdered sweetener: 1 tbsp.
- Vanilla extract: ½ tbsp.
- Coconut: ¼ cup finely shredded
- Whole almonds: 14

Directions:

1. Preheat a mini waffle maker if needed and grease it
2. In a mixing bowl, add all the chaffle ingredients
3. Mix them all well

4. Pour the mixture to the lower plate of the waffle maker and spread it evenly to cover the plate properly
5. Close the lid
6. Cooking for at least 4 minutes to get the desired crunch
7. Remove the chaffle from the heat and keep aside for around one minute
8. Make as many chaffles as your mixture and waffle maker allow
9. Except for almond, add all the filling ingredients in a bowl and mix well
10. Spread the filling on the chaffle and spread almonds on top with another chaffle at almonds – stack the chaffles and fillings like a cake and enjoy

Nutrition: Calories: 85 Fat: 0.5 g Protein: 4 g Carbs: 6 g Fiber: 4g

32. **Peanut Butter Keto Chaffle Cake**

Preparation Time: 5 minutes

Cooking Time: 10 minutes

Servings: 2

Ingredients:

For Chaffles:

- Egg: 1
- Peanut Butter: 2 tbsp. (sugar-free)
- Monkfruit: 2 tbsp.
- Baking powder: ¼ tsp.
- Peanut butter extract: ¼ tsp.
- Heavy whipping cream: 1 tsp.

For Peanut Butter Frosting:

- Monkfruit: 2 tsp.
- Cream cheese: 2 tbsp.
- Butter: 1 tbsp.
- Peanut butter: 1 tbsp. (sugar-free)
- Vanilla: ¼ tsp.

Directions:

1. Preheat a mini waffle maker if needed and grease it
2. In a mixing bowl, beat eggs and add all the chaffle ingredients
3. Mix them all well and pour the mixture to the lower plate of the waffle maker
4. Close the lid
5. Cooking for at least 4 minutes to get the desired crunch

6. Remove the chaffle from the heat and keep aside for around a few minutes
7. Make as many chaffles as your mixture and waffle maker allow
8. In a separate bowl, add all the frosting ingredients and whisk well to give it a uniform consistency
9. Assemble chaffles in a way that in between two chaffles you put the frosting and make the cake

Nutrition: Calories 214 Fat 8.6 g Saturated fat 1.5 g Carbohydrates 27.3 g Fiber 8.4 g Protein 8 g

33. Italian Cream Chaffle Cake

Preparation Time: 8 minutes

Cooking Time: 12 minutes

Servings: 3

Ingredients:

For Chaffle:

- Egg: 4
- Mozzarella cheese: ½ cup
- Almond flour: 1 tbsp.
- Coconut flour: 4 tbsp.
- Monkfruit sweetener: 1 tbsp.
- Vanilla extract: 1 tsp.
- Baking powder: 1 ½ tsp.
- Cinnamon powder: ½ tsp.
- Butter: 1 tbsp. (melted)
- Coconut: 1 tsp. (shredded)
- Walnuts: 1 tsp. (chopped)

For Italian Cream Frosting:

- Cream cheese: 4 tbsp.
- Butter: 2 tbsp.
- Vanilla: ½ tsp.
- Monkfruit sweetener: 2 tbs

Directions:

1. Blend eggs, cream cheese, sweetener, vanilla, coconut flour, melted butter, almond flour, and baking powder
2. Make the mixture creamy

3. Preheat a mini waffle maker if needed and grease it
4. Pour the mixture to the lower plate of the waffle maker
5. Close the lid
6. Cooking for at least 4 minutes to get the desired crunch
7. Remove the chaffle from the heat and keep aside to cool it
8. Make as many chaffles as your mixture and waffle maker allow
9. Garnish with shredded coconut and chopped walnuts

Nutrition: Calories 69 Fat 3.7 g Saturated fat 0.6 g Carbohydrates 7.1 g

Fiber 1.8 g Protein 2 g

34. Banana Cake Pudding Chaffle

Preparation Time: 10 minutes

Cooking Time: 1 hour

Servings: 2

Ingredients:

For Banana Chaffle:

- Cream cheese: 2 tbsp.
- Banana extract: 1 tsp.
- Mozzarella cheese: ¼ cup
- Egg: 1
- Sweetener: 2 tbsp.
- Almond flour: 4 tbsp.
- Baking powder: 1 tsp.

For Banana Pudding:

- Egg yolk: 1 large
- Powdered sweetener: 3 tbsp.
- Xanthan gum: ½ tsp.
- Heavy whipping cream: 1/2 cup
- Banana extract: ½ tsp.
- Salt: a pinch

Directions:

1. In a pan, add powdered sweetener, heavy cream, and egg yolk and whisk continuously so the mixture thickens
2. Simmer for a minute only
3. Add xanthan gum to the mixture and whisk again

4. Remove the pan from heat and add banana extract and salt and mix them all well
5. Shift the mixture to a glass dish and refrigerate the pudding
6. Preheat a mini waffle maker if needed and grease it
7. In a mixing bowl, add all the chaffle ingredients
8. Mix them all well and pour the mixture to the lower plate of the waffle maker
9. Close the lid
10. Cooking for at least 5 minutes to get the desired crunch
11. Remove the chaffle from the heat and keep aside for around a few minutes
12. Stack chaffles and pudding one by one to form a cake

Nutrition: Calories 187 Fat 16.7 g Saturated fat 4.1 g Carbohydrates 6.7 g Fiber 2 g Protein 3.3 g

35. Cream Coconut Chaffle Cake

Preparation Time: 20 minutes

Cooking Time: 1 hour 20 minutes (depends on your refrigerator)

Servings: 2

Ingredients:

For Chaffles:

- Egg: 2
- Powdered sweetener: 2 tbsp.
- Cream cheese: 2 tbsp.
- Vanilla extract: 1/2 tsp.
- Butter: 1 tbsp. (melted)
- Coconut: 2 tbsp. (shredded)
- Coconut extract: ½ tsp.

For Filling:

- Coconut: ¼ cup (shredded)
- Butter: 2 tsp.
- Monkfruit sweetener: 2 tbsp.
- Xanthan gum: ¼ tsp.
- Salt: a pinch
- Egg yolks: 2
- Almond: 1/3 cup unsweetened
- Coconut milk: 1/3 cup

For Garnishing:

- Whipped Cream: as per your taste
- Coconut: 1 tbsp. (shredded)

Directions:

1. Preheat a mini waffle maker if needed and grease it
2. In a mixing bowl, add all the chaffle ingredients
3. Mix them all well and pour the mixture to the lower plate of the waffle maker
4. Close the lid
5. Cooking for at least 4 minutes to get the desired crunch
6. Remove the chaffle from the heat and keep aside for around a few minutes
7. Make as many chaffles as your mixture and waffle maker allow
8. For the filling, in a small pan, cooking almond milk and coconut together on medium heat in such way that it only steams but doesn't boil
9. In another bowl, lightly whish egg yolks and add milk to it continuously
10. Heat the mixture so it thickens, again it must not boil
11. Add sweetener and whisk while adding Xanthan Gum bit by bit
12. Remove from heat and mix all the other ingredients
13. Mix well and refrigerate; the mixture will further thicken when cool
14. Assemble the prepared chaffles and cream on top of one another to make the cake-like shape
15. Garnish with coconuts and whipped cream at the end

Nutrition: Calories 299 Fat 24.7 g Saturated fat 5.1 g Carbohydrates 11.6 g Fiber 2.8 g Protein 7 g

36. Fluffy White Chaffles

Preparation time: 10 minutes

Cooking time: 5 minutes

Servings: 4 mini chaffles

Ingredients:

- 1 large egg
- 1 large egg white
- 2 tablespoons cream cheese
- ½ cup grated Mozzarella cheese
- 2 tablespoons coconut flour
- ¼ cup almond flour
- ¼ teaspoon vanilla extract
- ½ teaspoon baking powder
- ¼ cup Swerve

Directions:

1. Preheat the mini waffle maker.
2. Place the egg, egg white, cream cheese, and Mozzarella into a blender. Process until smooth. Add the remaining ingredients and process again.
3. Spoon one quarter of the batter into the waffle maker. Cooking for 2 to 4 minutes or until golden brown. Transfer the chaffle onto a cooling rack to cool. Repeat with the remaining batter.
4. Serve immediately.

Nutrition: Calories 224 Fat 18 g Saturated fat 3.9 g Carbohydrates 6.1 g Fiber 3.6 g Protein 10.6 g

37. Blueberry Keto Chaffle

Preparation time: 3 minutes

Cooking time: 15 minutes

Servings: 5

Ingredients:

- 2 eggs
- 1 cup Mozzarella cheese
- 2 tablespoons almond flour
- 2 teaspoons Swerve, plus additional for serving
- 1 teaspoon baking powder
- 1 teaspoon cinnamon
- 3 tablespoon blueberries
- Nonstick cooking spray

Directions:

1. Preheat the mini waffle maker.
2. Stir together the eggs, Mozzarella cheese, almond flour, Swerve, baking powder, cinnamon, and blueberries in a mixing bowl. Spray the waffle maker with nonstick cooking spray.
3. Pour in a little bit less than ¼ a cup of blueberry waffle batter at a time.
4. Close the lid and cooking the chaffle for 3 to 5 minutes. Check it at the 3-minute mark to see if it is crispy and brown. If it is not or it sticks to the top of the waffle maker, close the lid and cooking for an additional 1 to 2 minutes.
5. Serve sprinkled with additional Swerve.

Nutrition: Calories: 370 Protein: 36 g Carbohydrates: 14 g Fats: 19 g

38. <u>Keto Birthday Cake Chaffle Recipe with Sprinkles</u>

Preparation Time: 10 minutes

Cooking Time: 7 minutes

Servings: 4

Ingredients:

Ingredients for chaffle cake:

- 2 eggs
- 1/4 almond flour
- 1 cup coconut powder
- 1 cup melted butter
- 2 tablespoons cream cheese
- 1 teaspoon cake butter extract
- 1 tsp. vanilla extract
- 2 tsp. baking powder
- 2 teaspoons confectionery sweetener or monk fruit
- 1/4 teaspoon xanthan powder whipped cream

Vanilla frosting ingredients

- 1/2 cup heavy whipped cream
- 2 tablespoons sweetener or monk fruit
- 1/2 teaspoon vanilla extract

Directions:

1. The mini waffle maker is preheated.
2. Add all the ingredients of the chaffle cake in a medium-sized blender and blend it to the top until it is smooth and creamy. Allow only a minute to sit with the

batter. It may seem a little watery, but it's going to work well.

3. Add 2 to 3 tablespoons of batter to your waffle maker and cooking until golden brown for about 2 to 3 minutes.

4. Start to frost the whipped vanilla cream in a separate bowl.

5. Add all the ingredients and mix with a hand mixer until thick and soft peaks are formed by the whipping cream.

6. Until frosting your cake, allow the cake to cool completely. If you frost it too soon, the frosting will be melted.

7. Enjoy!

Nutrition: Calories: 138 Protein: 11 g Carbohydrates: 8 g Fats: 7 g

DESSERT CHAFFLE RECIPES

39. Italian Cream Chaffle Sandwich-cake

Preparation time: 8 minutes

Cooking Time: 20 Minutes

Servings: 2

Ingredients:

- 4 oz cream cheese, softened, at room temperature
- 4 eggs
- 1 Tbsp melted butter
- 1 tsp vanilla extract
- ½ tsp cinnamon
- 1 Tbsp monk fruit sweetener
- 4 Tbsp coconut flour
- 1 Tbsp almond flour
- 1½ teaspoons baking powder
- 1 Tbsp coconut, shredded and unsweetened
- 1 Tbsp walnuts, chopped

For the Italian cream frosting:

- 2 oz cream cheese, softened, at room temperature
- 2 Tbsp butter room temp
- 2 Tbsp monk fruit sweetener
- ½ tsp vanilla

Directions:

1. Combine cream cheese, eggs, melted butter, vanilla, sweetener, flours, and baking powder in a blender.
2. Add walnuts and coconut to the mixture.
3. Blend to get a creamy mixture.
4. Turn on waffle maker to heat and oil it with cooking spray.
5. Add enough batter to fill waffle maker. Cook for 2-3 minutes, until chaffles are done.
6. Remove and let them cool.
7. Mix all frosting ingredients in another bowl. Stir until smooth and creamy.
8. Frost the chaffles once they have cooled.
9. Top with cream and more nuts.

Nutrition Calories: 200 Fat: 8g Carbohydrates: 3g Protein: 26g

40. Whipping Cream Chaffle

Preparation time: 5 minutes

Cooking Time: 8 Minutes

Servings: 2

Ingredients:

- 1 organic egg, beaten
- 1 tablespoon heavy whipping cream
- 2 tablespoons sugar-free peanut butter powder
- 2 tablespoons Erythritol
- ¼ teaspoon organic baking powder
- ¼ teaspoon peanut butter extract

Directions:

1. Preheat a mini waffle iron and then grease it.
2. In a medium bowl, place all ingredients and with a fork, mix until well combined.
3. Place half of the mixture into preheated waffle iron and cook for about 4 minutes or until golden brown.
4. Repeat with the remaining mixture.
5. Serve warm.

Nutrition Calories: 464 Fat: 34g Carbohydrates: 3g Protein: 34g

41. Cinnamon Pumpkin Chaffles

Preparation time: 8 minutes

Cooking Time: 16 Minutes

Servings: 2

Ingredients:

- 2 organic eggs
- 2/3 cup Mozzarella cheese, shredded
- 3 tablespoons sugar-free pumpkin puree
- 3 teaspoons almond flour
- 2 teaspoons granulated Erythritol
- 2 teaspoons ground cinnamon

Directions:

1. Preheat a mini waffle iron and then grease it.
2. In a medium bowl, place all ingredients and with a fork, mix until well combined.
3. Place half of the mixture into preheated waffle iron and cook for about 4 minutes or until golden brown.
4. Repeat with the remaining mixture.
5. Serve warm.

Nutrition Calories: 200 Fat: 11g Carbohydrates: 6g Protein: 11g

42. Red Velvet Chaffles

Preparation time: 5 minutes

Cooking Time: 8 Minutes

Servings: 2

Ingredients:

- 2 tablespoons cacao powder
- 2 tablespoons erythritol
- 1 organic egg, beaten
- 2 drops super red food coloring
- ¼ teaspoon organic baking powder
- 1 tablespoon heavy whipping cream

Directions:

1. Preheat a mini waffle iron and then grease it.
2. In a medium bowl, put all ingredients and with a fork, mix until well combined.
3. Place half of the mixture into preheated waffle iron and cook for about 4 minutes.
4. Repeat with the remaining mixture.
5. Serve warm.

Nutrition Calories: 325 Fat: 24g Carbohydrates: 3g Protein: 16g

43. <u>Mayonnaise Chaffles</u>

Preparation time: 5 minutes

Cooking Time: 10 Minutes

Servings: 3

Ingredients:

- 1 large organic egg, beaten1 tablespoon mayonnaise
- 2 tablespoons almond flour
- 1/8 teaspoon organic baking powder
- 1 teaspoon water2–4 drops liquid stevia

Directions:

1. Preheat a mini waffle iron and then grease it.
2. In a medium bowl, put all ingredients and with a fork, mix until well combined. Place half of the mixture into preheated waffle iron and cook for about 4–5 minutes.
3. Repeat with the remaining mixture.
4. Serve warm.

Nutrition Calories: 502 Fat: 39g Carbohydrates: 01.8g Protein: 34g

44. Chocolate Peanut Butter Chaffle

Preparation time: 5 minutes

Cooking Time: 10 Minutes

Servings: 2

Ingredients:

- ½ cup shredded mozzarella cheese
- 1 Tbsp cocoa powder
- 2 Tbsp powdered sweetener
- 2 Tbsp peanut butter
- ½ tsp vanilla
- 1 egg
- 2 Tbsp crushed peanuts
- 2 Tbsp whipped cream
- ¼ cup sugar-free chocolate syrup

Directions:

1. Combine mozzarella, egg, vanilla, peanut butter, cocoa powder, and sweetener in a bowl.
2. Add in peanuts and mix well.
3. Turn on waffle maker and oil it with cooking spray.
4. Pour one half of the batter into waffle maker and cook for minutes, then transfer to a plate.
5. Top with whipped cream, peanuts, and sugar-free chocolate syrup.

Nutrition: Calories 112 Fat 10 g Cholesterol 0 mg Carbohydrates 8 g Sugar 5 g Fiber 2 g Protein 2 g

45. <u>Lemon Curd Chaffles</u>

Preparation time: 5 minutes

Cooking Time: 5 Minutes

Servings: 1

Ingredients:

- 3 large eggs
- 4 oz cream cheese, softened
- 1 Tbsp low carb sweetener
- 1 tsp vanilla extract
- ¾ cup mozzarella cheese, shredded
- 3 Tbsp coconut flour
- 1 tsp baking powder
- 1/3 tsp salt

For the lemon curd:

- ½-1 cup water
- 5 egg yolks
- ½ cup lemon juice
- ½ cup powdered sweetener
- 2 Tbsp fresh lemon zest
- 1 tsp vanilla extract
- Pinch of salt
- 8 Tbsp cold butter, cubed

Directions:

1. Pour water into a saucepan and heat over medium until it reaches a soft boil. Start with ½ cup and add more if needed.

2. Whisk yolks, lemon juice, lemon zest, powdered sweetener, vanilla, and salt in a medium heat-proof bowl. Leave to set for 5-6 minutes.
3. Place bowl onto saucepan and heat. The bowl shouldn't be touching water.
4. Whisk mixture for 8-10 minutes, or until it begins to thicken.
5. Add butter cubes and whisk for 7 minutes, until it thickens.
6. When it lightly coats the back of a spoon, remove from heat.
7. Refrigerate until cool, allowing it to continue thickening.
8. Turn on waffle maker to heat and oil it with cooking spray.
9. Add baking powder, coconut flour, and salt in a small bowl. Mix well and set aside.
10. Add eggs, cream cheese, sweetener, and vanilla in a separate bowl. Using a hand beater, beat until frothy.
11. Add mozzarella to egg mixture and beat again.
12. Add dry ingredients and mix until well-combined.
13. Add batter to waffle maker and cook for 3-4 minutes.
14. Transfer to a plate and top with lemon curd before serving.

Nutrition: Calories 126 Fat 8 g Cholesterol 0 mg Carbohydrate 14 g Sugar 4 g Fiber 2 g Protein 3 g Sodium 108 mg Calcium 55 mg Phosphorus 70 mg Potassium 298 mg

46. Walnut Pumpkin Chaffles

Preparation time: 5 minutes

Cooking Time: 10 Minutes

Servings: 2

Ingredients:

- 1 organic egg, beaten
- ½ cup Mozzarella cheese, shredded
- 2 tablespoons almond flour
- 1 tablespoon sugar-free pumpkin puree
- 1 teaspoon Erythritol
- ¼ teaspoon ground cinnamon
- 2 tablespoons walnuts, toasted and chopped

Directions:

1. Preheat a mini waffle iron and then grease it.
2. In a bowl, place all ingredients except walnuts and beat until well combined.
3. Fold in the walnuts.
4. Place half of the mixture into preheated waffle iron and cook for about 5 minutes or until golden brown.
5. Repeat with the remaining mixture.
6. Serve warm.

Nutrition: Calories 146 Fat 5 g Cholesterol 35 mg Carbohydrates 8 g Sugar 4 g Fiber 0 g Protein 16 g Sodium 58 mg Calcium 18 mg Phosphorus 125 mg Potassium 212 mg

47. Protein Mozzarella Chaffles

Preparation time: 8 minutes

Cooking Time: 20 Minutes

Servings: 2

Ingredients:

- ½ scoop unsweetened protein powder
- 2 large organic eggs
- ½ cup Mozzarella cheese, shredded
- 1 tablespoon Erythritol
- ¼ teaspoon organic vanilla extract

Directions:

1. Preheat a mini waffle iron and then grease it.
2. In a medium bowl, place all ingredients and with a fork, mix until well combined.
3. Place ¼ of the mixture into preheated waffle iron and cook for about 4-5 minutes or until golden brown.
4. Repeat with the remaining mixture.
5. Serve warm.

Nutrition: Calories 400 Fat 21 g Cholesterol 0 mg Carbohydrates 46 g Sugar 2 g Fiber 3 g Protein 11 g Sodium 6 mg Calcium 64 mg Phosphorus 113 mg Potassium 202 mg

48. Chocolate Chips Peanut Butter Chaffles

Preparation time: 5 minutes

Cooking Time: 8 Minutes

Servings: 4

Ingredients:

- 1 organic egg, beaten
- ¼ cup Mozzarella cheese, shredded
- 2 tablespoons creamy peanut butter
- 1 tablespoon almond flour
- 1 tablespoon granulated Erythritol
- 1 teaspoon organic vanilla extract
- 1 tablespoon 70% dark chocolate chips

Directions:

1. Preheat a mini waffle iron and then grease it.
2. In a bowl, place all ingredients except chocolate chips and beat until well combined.
3. Gently, fold in the chocolate chips.
4. Place half of the mixture into preheated waffle iron and cook for about minutes or until golden brown.
5. Repeat with the remaining mixture.
6. Serve warm.

Nutrition: Calories 47 Fat 1 g Cholesterol 0 g Carbohydrates 8 g Sugar 6 g Fiber 2 g Protein 2 g Sodium 104 mg Calcium 36 mg Phosphorus 52 mg Potassium 298 mg

49. Dessert Pumpkin Chaffles

Preparation time: 5 minutes

Cooking Time: 12 Minutes

Servings: 3

Ingredients:

- 1 organic egg, beaten
- ½ cup Mozzarella cheese, shredded
- 1½ tablespoon homemade pumpkin puree
- ½ teaspoon Erythritol
- ½ teaspoon organic vanilla extract
- ¼ teaspoon pumpkin pie spice

Directions:

1. Preheat a mini waffle iron and then grease it.
2. In a bowl, place all the ingredients and beat until well combined.
3. Place ¼ of the mixture into preheated waffle iron and cook for about 4-6 minutes or until golden brown.
4. Repeat with the remaining mixture.
5. Serve warm.

Nutrition: Calories 300 Fat 19 g Cholesterol 0 mg Carbohydrates 34 g Sugar 11 g Fiber 5 g Protein 6 g Sodium 6 mg Calcium 30 mg Phosphorus 144 mg Potassium 296 mg

50. Lemon Chaffles

Preparation time: 5 minutes

Cooking Time: 10 Minutes

Servings: 2

Ingredients:

- 1 organic egg, beaten
- 1-ounce cream cheese, softened
- 2 tablespoons almond flour
- 1 tablespoon fresh lemon juice
- 2 teaspoons Erythritol
- ½ teaspoon fresh lemon zest, grated
- ¼ teaspoon organic baking powder
- Pinch of salt
- ½ teaspoon powdered Erythritol

Directions:

1. Preheat a mini waffle iron and then grease it.
2. In a bowl, place all ingredients except the powdered Erythritol and beat until well combined.
3. Place half of the mixture into preheated waffle iron and cook for about 5 minutes or until golden brown.
4. Repeat with the remaining mixture.
5. Serve warm with the sprinkling of powdered Erythritol.

Nutrition: Calories: 51 Fat: 2g Carb: 9g Phosphorus: 33mg Potassium: 98mg Sodium: 78mg Protein: 2g

CONCLUSION

Thank you for reaching the end of this book.

Have you enjoyed these recipes? I would love to hear your experience. You may leave a comment to let me know. I would really appreciate it.

Here are some basics about Ketogenic Diet that I would like to share with you.

Ketogenic Diet had been used for decades to treat patients with epilepsy and is still in use today. The diet has also been used to help people lose weight, and it's been shown that a ketogenic diet can cause weight loss even when calories are not restricted.

The keto diet is one that consists of eating lots of fat, moderate protein, and low carbs. It's more common for people to go into ketosis as long as they restrict their carbohydrate intake. The ketogenic diet can help many people lose a lot of weight.

There are lots of benefits to being in a state of ketosis. A person can experience less hunger, and cravings for carbs can be lessened while in the state of ketosis. This diet is impossible to stop once a person is in it because making an adjustment back to eating carbs would cause them to get out of this state, which isn't something that they want.

The main goal of a ketogenic diet is to put the body into a metabolic state called ketosis so that you're able to burn fat for energy instead of glucose.

Here are some concerns about ketogenic diet that I want you to be aware of:

First, the ketogenic diet is very restrictive. This means that it's difficult to follow if you're used to eating a lot of carbohydrates. It is possible to have a decent amount of carbs while following a keto diet, but some people don't want this to be the case. The biggest thing that you'll need to do when you start eating this way is to cut out the sugar, grains and starchy foods.

Next, it's hard for many people to stick with this diet for a long period of time. People might assume that they can eat whatever they want as long as they are in a state of ketosis, but this isn't true at all. Eating keto-friendly foods is still a challenge for some individuals, and since the diet can be difficult to stick with, it's not considered to be a long-term solution for weight loss.

Finally, just because someone is in a state of ketosis doesn't mean that they are going to lose a lot of weight. Ketones can cause weight loss in some people because the body will burn off fat instead of burning off glucose. This makes it easy for people to drop pounds if they're only eating fat, but it's not equally as simple for them to shed pounds if they're eating carbs and protein too.

I hope that these book about keto chaffle recipes had helped you and somehow made your ketogenic diet journey a lot easier. Thank you so much for reading this book.

CPSIA information can be obtained
at www.ICGtesting.com
Printed in the USA
LVHW021732010421
683230LV00002B/78